Parent-Tested Ways to Grow Your Child's Confidence

Silvana Clark

 **Meadowbrook Press**

Distributed by Simon & Schuster
New York

Library of Congress Cataloging-in Publication Data
Clark, Silvana.
    Parent-tested ways to grow your child's confidence / Silvana Clark.
        p. cm.
    ISBN 0-88166-369-7 (Meadowbrook) ISBN 0-671-31823-3 (Simon
    & Schuster)
        1. Child rearing. 2. Self-confidence in children. 3. Parent and
    child. I. Title.
    HQ769 .C6124 2000
    649'.7—dc21   00-024913

Managing Editor: Christine Zuchora-Walske
Copyeditor: Joseph Gredler
Proofreader: Megan McGinnis
Production Manager: Paul Woods
Desktop Publishing: Danielle White
Cover Art: Jone Hallmark

Published by Meadowbrook Press, 5451 Smetana Drive, Minnetonka,
Minnesota 55343
www.meadowbrookpress.com

BOOK TRADE DISTRIBUTION by Simon & Schuster, a division of
Simon and Schuster, Inc., 1230 Avenue of the Americas, New York
NY 10020

04 03 02 01 00   10 9 8 7 6 5 4 3 2 1

Printed in the United States of America

Contents

Introduction v

Chapter 1:
Speak Supportively 1

Chapter 2:
Encourage with Your Actions 29

Chapter 3:
Take Time Out for Togetherness 65

Chapter 4:
Keep Close When You're Apart 81

Chapter 5:
Express Your Love with Words and Art . . 99

Chapter 6:
Confront Challenges with Courage 125

Chapter 7:
Invent and Enjoy Special Occasions . . . 141

Dedication

This book is dedicated to my two self-confident daughters, Trina and Sondra, and to every child who might need encouragement.

Acknowledgments

A special thanks to the "expert" moms and dads who shared their experiences in this book. I've enjoyed talking to you at workshops over the years, and I've appreciated how eagerly you've shared methods of helping children develop self-confidence. I'd also like to thank my agent, Linda Konner, who was always quick with e-mail responses and never made me feel like a pest. Finally, I'd like to thank the staff at Meadowbrook Press who handled each step of the production process in a courteous, professional manner. A special thanks to Steve Linders who patiently sat through my lengthy phone calls. Thank you all!

Introduction

I recently bought a package of wildflower seeds after being enticed by the brilliant-colored photographs on the cover. The instructions stated "Simply toss these seeds on the ground and water. Within weeks you'll have a gorgeous garden filled with a wide variety of colorful wildflowers." This was my first attempt at gardening, so I dutifully scattered the seeds and sprinkled them with water. One week passed but there was no sign of growth. Another week passed and the ground still contained only dirt and weeds. After five weeks, I realized my gorgeous wildflower garden wasn't going to materialize.

I complained to a green-thumbed friend who proceeded to lecture me on the substantial work involved in growing a flower garden. My eyes glazed over as she explained the importance of preparing the soil, controlling pests, selecting the seeds according to available sunshine, and so on. She made me realize that gardening takes serious time and effort, but she also reminded me that the rewards are worth it.

Children also need a great deal of time and effort to help them realize their potential. As parents and caregivers, we have an enormous responsibility to help children develop a healthy outlook on life. Successful gardeners carefully decide where to plant their tomatoes, and parents must attentively establish methods of nurturing their children's self-confidence. For example, if your daughter is trying out for the school play, you could do some role-playing to help her understand what it might be like to stand in front of an audience and speak lines in a clear, loud voice. If your son has a sensitive spirit, you could let him overhear you telling Grandma how he befriended the new kid at school.

As a professional speaker, I enjoy the privilege of meeting parents from all over the world who share wonderfully creative ways of helping children learn self-confidence. Parents eagerly tell me what's worked for them—and what hasn't! We laugh about some of the well-intentioned techniques that backfired. One father told a story about a complicated seven-step process he'd learned at a lecture. Naturally, the lecturer had no children of his own! I prefer to focus on tested strategies that have worked for the real experts: parents. You'll hear from moms and dads just starting out with a single toddler at home, to more experienced parents who are now working with prisoners at San Quentin. It's been my pleasure to hear their stories over the years, and I hope they will be equally inspiring to you.

Silvana

Speak Supportively

Pet Phrase

Develop a special phrase or saying for your child shared by only the two of you. Repeat it on a regular basis to make your child feel distinguished.

From the time my son was two, I would tuck him in each night and say, "You're the best son I ever had." He was four before he caught on and said, "Mom, I'm the only son you ever had." I would reply, "If I had a hundred sons, you'd still be the best." Today, my son is twenty-four, and I still tell him, "You're the best son I ever had!"

—Catherine Jewell, trainer and speaker

Positive Reinforcement

When your children do something commendable, tell someone else about it within their hearing. "That was so nice of you to teach Melissa how to play the game, I'm going to call Grandma and tell her what you did!" Make sure your child can hear the conversation.

When my energetic, headstrong two-year-old cooperates by putting her dirty clothes in the hamper or by sharing her toy with a friend, I make a point of calling her dad at work. If I get his answering machine, I leave a message such as "Hi. Julie helped me today by putting all her toys in the toy box." Julie beams, and her dad compliments her again when he comes home.

—Tired mother of a two-year-old

Pet Names

Choose pet names for your children. Select ones they like and make sure to use them only at home if they embarrass your kids. Your first-grader probably won't mind you saying "See you later, Sweet Pea" when you drop her off at school, but your ten-year-old will likely prefer a simple "Bye, Sandy."

I have pet names for each of my kids and use them often. I call my toddler "Little One" even though he'll probably wind up much bigger than the rest of us. I call my daughter "Precious" not because of what she does or how she looks, but because of who she is.

—Kirsten Andrews, mother of Becca and Jonathon

Reasons for Rules

Take time to explain the reasons behind family rules. Children naturally want to know why they have to do things a certain way. You might find yourself saying, "Don't touch that vase!" When your child asks, "Why?" try to avoid responding, "Because I said so!" A simple explanation will often result in a more compliant child.

While waiting in line at the grocery store, my four-year-old began hanging on a metal dividing rail. I showed her how the ends weren't bolted to the wall and explained to her that the rail could fall down and she could be injured. The clerk said, "I've worked here for three years. At least once a day, a parent tells her kid to get off that rail. You're the first one to ever explain the reason to your child."

—*Mother and bank teller*

Teach Empathy

Let your children hear you empathize with people, especially those in need. Ask your children how they would feel if they were lost like the girl they saw on the news. If you drive by a homeless person, explain to your kids how and why some people live on the streets.

When my son was five, we bought a book of Norman Rockwell paintings. My son loved to sit and talk about each picture. He'd describe how the person in the picture was feeling, why the little boy was smiling, or how the little girl felt on her first day of school. The pictures showed people exhibiting a wide range of emotions, and the images weren't too graphic for him.

—Mother and librarian

Optimistic Self-Talk

Encourage healthy self-talk in your family. Studies show optimistic people have the ability to think in an upbeat manner because their internal voices are positive. Instead of allowing your kids to think "I'm no good at math," encourage them to think "I'll learn my multiplication tables, and then math will be easy."

When our daughter Lauren started to come home frustrated from first grade, we wrote a self-talk script for her to read every morning. She read phrases such as "I am a winner; I expect to win," "I make friends easily," and "I don't worry about bad things others say, because I am special and God has a special plan for me." This helped her tremendously.

—*Dan and Lynn Tegtmeyer, proud parents*

Voice Mail

If your children arrive home before you do, record a phone message to greet their arrival. Many children rush to the answering machine or phone to check voice mail as soon as they get home. Your kids will appreciate your encouraging words or humor. Compliment your children on how well they prepared for school that morning or tell them a joke.

I used a book of knock-knock riddles to create humorous answering-machine messages for my kids. I'd say "Knock Knock" and leave time for my daughter to answer "Who's There?" I'd continue with the joke, pausing once again for her reply. My daughter got a kick out of talking back to the machine.

—Mother and computer programmer

Kids to the Rescue

Your kids would probably object if you tried to change a word of their best-loved stories. However, when you read less familiar ones or create your own, incorporate your child's name into the role of the main character. Kids enjoy hearing a story in which they play a major role.

When my children ask me to tell them a story, I make up a lengthy tale with them as the central characters. They are the heroes who save the town and townspeople. They love being in the story.

—Justin Mitchell, social administrator

Reward Hard Work

Choose a time when your children are diligently doing their chores. Give them a hug and say "I appreciate how well you're vacuuming the car. Why don't you go play while I finish your jobs." They won't believe you at first, but they'll gradually learn that hard work is always rewarded.

Once a month or so, I'll surprise my children by completing one of their chores. I've discovered they work harder knowing there's a possibility I'll take over. I was shocked last week when my nine-year-old said, "Mom, you're doing a good job dusting. Read a magazine while I finish!"

—Still-in-shock mother

Value Your Children's Opinions

Promote self-esteem in your children by encouraging them to express their views. Take time to ask thought-provoking questions like "How do you think the substitute teacher felt when the class didn't listen to her directions?" or "What can we do to help the neighbor family whose dog was hit by a car?" Listen carefully to their answers. Children who are taught their views are important learn to express their opinions in a positive way.

During dinner, I often read a short article from the daily paper. I select letters to Ann Landers, letters to the editor, captions underneath photographs, and so on. Every family member has a chance to express an opinion without being interrupted. It makes for lively dinner conversation.

—Dad and postal worker

Here's to Your Kids!

Propose a toast to your children. Make it simple or long-winded—whatever you like. Your kids will enjoy clinking their glasses while you say something profound like "Every once in a while, an athlete demonstrates her true sense of skill and endurance. Here's a toast to the only person in our family blessed with the ability to Hula-Hoop for two minutes and seventeen seconds...Megan Copeland!" Don't forget to clap and cheer!

Whenever our family goes out to restaurants, for some reason we feel compelled to toast each other. My husband always makes a semimushy toast to me, and then the kids come up with toasts for each other. Some are too gross to be repeated!

—Embarrassed mother of three outgoing children

Celebrate the Last Day of School

Many parents celebrate the first day of the school year. Why not celebrate the last day, too? Commemorate your children's completion of another academic year by serving special snacks or presenting small gifts. Ask your children to describe the skills they learned and to explain any changes they've noticed in themselves since the beginning of the school year.

I bring one Mylar balloon with "Congratulations" painted on it to the last day of school to celebrate each of my children's advancement to the next grade level. They love it.

—Kathy Moreno, stay-at-home mother of three children

Show a Little Courtesy

In the professional world, businesspeople treat customers with courtesy and respect. But frequently at home they forget even the simplest courtesies with their children. Make an effort to say "Please" and "Thank you" to your kids on a regular basis. Also, try not to interrupt them, even when they're telling a drawn-out story about the cafeteria food fight.

I treat my children as valued customers. This technique is not about spoiling children; it's about fulfilling our basic needs to feel welcomed, important, understood, and comforted.

—*Tom Lagana, coauthor of* Chicken Soup for the Prisoner's Soul

Frame a Crisis Objectively

Reconstruct your children's problems in ways they can understand. After giving them time to vent their frustrations, restate the situation in clear, factual terms. This teaches them the ability to look at their problems objectively.

Sondra came home from school one day moaning, "I had a horrible day!" After a snack, we went through her day hour by hour. I took notes while she described how she began with her favorite breakfast (lentil soup), how she wore a new shirt, how she got to ride her bike to school, how well she did on her spelling test, and how much she liked her nice teachers. She eventually realized her "horrible" day consisted of five minutes of minor conflict over a tetherball game.

—Silvana, mother of two girls

One Good Thing

Find at least one heartening thing to say to your children every day. Acknowledge them for hanging up their backpacks, smiling at an elderly neighbor, gently petting a kitten, and so on. This helps them focus on the good things they do.

My three boys were raised in a single-parent home. Their dad was killed in a car accident when they were two, six, and eight years old. The most important thing I did for them was to provide lots of praise and love. Today, they are successful adults. They attribute their success to a parent who supported them no matter what they ventured into.

—Ingrid Dosta, instructional assistant

Draw the Line

Let your children know that certain family rules are set in stone. Most parents agree there's no room for discussion when it comes to seat belts. The same goes for bike helmets or saying mean things about others. Children gain a sense of security knowing there are absolute standards of behavior in their family.

We have certain non-negotiable rules in our house. The kids are expected to follow these rules without arguing. Everything else is open to discussion. Occasionally, my three-year-old will ask, "Is eating broccoli negotiable or non-negotiable?" If I say it's negotiable, she uses her skills to argue her position. However, if I say, "This issue is non-negotiable," my kids know I mean it.

—Mother of three persuasive children

Interactive Television

Watch TV with your children and discuss with them what you see. Occasionally mute the commercials and ask your kids to guess what the actors are saying. Your children will probably begin to notice the exaggerated facial expressions and enticing graphics. You might discuss the ways in which advertisers cleverly encourage us to buy items we don't really need. Eventually, your children will learn to control their buying impulses and will watch TV with increased critical awareness.

When my children watch TV, I make a point of showing them the hype that goes into each commercial. They've become smart consumers because we've discussed how advertisers use gimmicks to sell products.

—Dad and chemist

Introduce Your Children Properly

Introduce your children to strangers the same way you would introduce a coworker or friend. Also, teach your children the proper way to acknowledge an introduction. Show them how to shake hands, make eye contact, and greet people respectfully. Adults will, in turn, comment on your kids' good manners, which will further enhance your children's self-confidence.

I always introduce my daughter by saying, "This is Sondra, my daughter." The word order is important because the statement shows that she is foremost an individual, and she is also my daughter.

—Allan, father of two girls

Reasonable Rules

Try to establish reasonable rules and expectations for your children. Ten-year-olds shouldn't have to be reminded to buckle their seat belts. If children understand what is expected of them, they will usually live up to those expectations. Trusting your kids to do the right thing will build their self-confidence.

My parents developed my self-esteem by telling me, "Become someone! Move out and get a job!" They gave me one year after I graduated from high school to find a job and a place to live. Thank goodness. They helped me learn to take care of myself. Life waits for no one.

—Aaron Callan, college student

"I Love You"

Never forget the fundamental confidence-booster: telling your children you love them. A pat on the shoulder, a hug, or a simple "I love you" conveys to your kids how much you care for them and how important they are.

I always try to hug my two boys and tell them "I love you" before they leave for school. If I'm too busy to initiate it, they do. I also write notes on their lunch napkins expressing my love for them. But mostly I tell them "I love you" on a regular basis.

—*Maggie Rody, mom and interior decorator*

Simple Praise

Make an effort to acknowledge the good things your children do. Perhaps they wipe their feet without being reminded, or they empty the dishwasher without being asked. We all respond effectively to praise. Whenever possible, be specific about what your kids have done well. Instead of only saying "Good job," try to say "Good job wiping up the dog's spilled water."

I keep a Polaroid camera on the kitchen counter. Whenever I see my child doing something positive, I yell, "Stop! Hold that position!" I take a picture and put it on the refrigerator inside a frame labeled "Look who we caught being good!"

—*Snap-happy mom in Philadelphia*

Listen First

Sometimes the best thing parents can do is keep quiet. When children need to talk, parents should make sure to listen first before giving advice. Your children might surprise you by figuring out a solution on their own.

Children desperately need to be heard. You don't always need to fix the problem—just hear them out. As a volunteer at San Quentin the past seven years, I've learned so much about little boys trapped inside men's bodies. They have so few communication skills. I've found they respond best to people who listen, encourage, and believe in them—things that should have been done during their childhood.

—Normandie Fallon, mom, nurse, and prison ministry volunteer

Encourage Hobbies

Encourage your children to develop hobbies. Even if you're bored reading the science fiction that your daughter loves so much, ask her about the books she's reading. Discuss what she finds appealing and listen to her insights.

My eight-year-old son enjoys gardening. When he brings home a good report card or performs some other praiseworthy act, we let him choose a reward (except for candy or toys). He usually picks a gardening book or a trip to a greenhouse to buy plants. I'm excited that he's acquiring skills and knowledge that will be useful to him later in life. I believe developing children's interests increases their self-esteem.

—Kristine Savage, single parent

Welcome to the Podium!

Studies have shown that the fear of public speaking is the number one phobia in the United States. So, whenever opportunities arise, encourage your children to speak before groups of relatives or friends. The confidence gained through public speaking will enhance their self-esteem.

We created a special camper-and-parent panel to talk to new families about summer camp. The girls were treated as distinguished guests—complete with name tags, water, snacks, and official introductions. They were given the opportunity to talk before the group about how great camp was. It built them up and also promoted our camp.

—Carol Culbertson, camp director, Freedom Valley Girl Scouts

Icebreakers

Sometimes children need help getting to know people in new social situations. Discuss the circumstances ahead of time and ask your kids for ideas. Work together to come up with concrete strategies like "When you arrive at the first Boy Scout meeting, look for another new boy and sit by him." Practical tips help children cope with potentially stressful situations.

My two children were apprehensive about attending overnight camp and feeling "like a number." I sent the entire camp ice pops for rest hour as a get-to-know-you gift from Cait and Will. This helped break the ice.

—Carol Solis, photographer

Appreciate Your Children's Ideas

Acknowledge your children whenever they teach you something. Appreciative comments like "I never would have thought to use strips of plastic bags for a kite tail—that was a good idea!" reinforce your children's self-esteem.

When our son started to drive, I learned some things from him that improved my own driving. Each time he switched lanes, he did a head check for a car in his blind spot. I said, "Wow, Brandon, I'm learning some great driving tips from you." That technique has been a lifesaver.

—*Tom Lagana, coauthor of* Chicken Soup for the Prisoner's Soul

Encourage
with Your
Actions

Offer Kids Choices

Give your children the opportunity to make choices. When they're fairly young, let them choose between the red socks and the pink ones. As they get older, let them choose between piano lessons and art classes. Children gain confidence by making decisions and experiencing the consequences of those decisions.

When Sondra was two, her grandmother gave her a fluffy square-dance-type petticoat. She loved it so much that she couldn't bear to hide it under her dress. For weeks, she insisted on wearing the petticoat over her dress or pants whenever we went out in public. People flashed me bemused looks, but I figured since it wasn't a safety issue, why not let her enjoy flouncing through childhood?

—Silvana, mother of two girls

Alone Time

Children with healthy self-esteem feel comfortable by themselves. They occasionally enjoy reading quietly, playing a game alone, or simply daydreaming. If possible, designate a special time for your kids to spend by themselves.

Lindi was three when she stopped taking naps, so I taught her to enjoy "Lindi's special time." At a certain time each day, she went to her room and entertained herself. She happily occupied herself with crayons, books, dolls, or a new toy. Today, she's quite content spending occasional time apart from friends and roommates.

—Becky Holmquist, teacher

Keepsake Box

Parents can't imagine the day their toddlers will leave home. Keep precious memories alive by collecting report cards, kindergarten pictures of toothless smiles, and other precious keepsakes in a special box. Make duplicates or copies whenever possible. When your children are ready to leave home, you'll have a wonderful treasure chest of memories to give them.

Ever since my children were little, I've collected duplicate sets of photographs in boxes so my kids will have their own sets to take with them when they move out.

—Rhonda Lennon, medical receptionist and Tupperware manager

Inexpensive Activities

Broaden your children's world with free or inexpensive activities. Take a tip from the Brownies, who offer "Try It" badges to expose girls to a variety of potential interests. Attend community theater productions, try a free class at the local craft store, or take a different route driving to the library.

We initiated an "educational experiences" program in which each family member had to plan an original, inexpensive activity for the entire family. We experienced senior-citizen craft shows, vegetarian food festivals, and even a Mexican hairless dog show! Our two girls enjoy trying new activities because of the success of our "educational experiences."

—Silvana, mother of two girls

Visual Keepsakes

If you observe your kids designing an elaborate structure with blocks or notice them drawing a particularly interesting picture, take time to record the event. Commemorate the creation of their masterpiece by videotaping the entire activity or by taking pictures of the various stages of creation.

My children loved building forts. We always seemed to have forts in various stages of development throughout the house and backyard. Whenever they made an especially creative fort, I'd take a picture and put it in our special photo album called "Amazing Forts by Sarah and Brandon."

—Mother of two future architects

The Little Things You Do

It's the small, unexpected things you do that frequently make the biggest impact on your children. If time permits, serve your kids a simple breakfast in bed before school. Add a flower or small stuffed animal to decorate their serving trays and read a favorite story while they eat.

It's always hard to rouse my children on the first Monday in spring after daylight-saving time has begun. My kids' bodies tell them they deserve another hour of sleep. To make getting up easier, I play soft music and bring them fruit and toast to eat in bed. It helps them start the morning on an upbeat note.

—Mother of a seven- and nine-year-old

Attend Social Events

Try to attend your children's school and social events. Your kids feel a tremendous sense of pride seeing you in the audience during their talent show.

Even though my dad was going through chemotherapy and his immune system was extremely susceptible to illness, he walked with me to the front of a large crowd on my high-school Senior Recognition Day. He was so proud to be my father that he risked his health to let everyone know I was his little girl. I felt like the happiest person in the gym that day.

—*Tara Barnes, college student*

Make an Activities List

Children with strong self-esteem usually know how to fill their free time. You can contribute by encouraging them to make a list of activities that will help them stay busy and feel happy. The next time they complain, "I'm bo-o-o-r-r-ed!" you can simply point to the list and suggest an activity.

I posted a list of my children's favorite activities on the refrigerator door to provide structure for their free time. The list gave them ideas about what they could do next. Instead of complaining, my kids merely glance at the list and begin a project. They are especially proud to have written it themselves.

—Teacher and mother in Wisconsin

Let Creativity Roam

Nurture creativity in your children. Look for possibilities in their wild ideas. If they want to create a unique flavor of ice cream or make their own skateboard, provide encouragement and assistance, but also try to stay out of their way. Let them know it's acceptable to have different ideas. We often discourage creativity by saying something like "You can't make the solar-system model out of fruit. Use Styrofoam balls so it looks nice."

My daughter is a free thinker. When her class was supposed to write a poem about spring, she wrote about how the garbage can smelled when filled with cut grass. I had to learn to respect and encourage her creative thoughts, which was hard for me.

—Conservative, mundane dad of a creative daughter

Loving Trinkets

Your children enjoy tangible reminders that you think they're wonderful. Keep a supply of special trinkets hidden away. (Easier said than done!) Every now and then, write a loving note, attach it to the trinket, and place it on their pillow or in their sock drawer. Part of their fun will be finding the gift in unexpected places.

I have a bag of ten thousand red hearts, each about the size of a pencil eraser. My children love it when these hearts show up in backpacks, lunches, underwear, and so on as a reminder that I love them.

—Carol Solis, photographer

Kids Can Teach

Encourage your children to share their skills with others. Is your daughter a whiz at math? Maybe she'd like to tutor your neighbor's second grader. Encourage your older son to teach his younger sister how to tie her shoes. Children gain confidence when they teach their skills to others.

Fourth- and fifth-graders at Silver Beach Elementary in Bellingham, Washington, participate in a "tech tutor" program. They spend an hour each week teaching senior citizens basic computer skills and ways to use the Internet. Students improve their patience and communication skills. One youngster observed a few of the residents picking up a mouse and trying to use it like a remote control. Before long, though, the seniors were surfing and sending e-mail.

—Dar New, librarian, Silver Beach School

Kids Can Help with Adult Projects

Help your children feel needed by asking them to help out on *real* adult projects. These tasks should be different from the regular chores kids do around the house. You could ask your children to walk an elderly neighbor's dog, type your Christmas card list on the computer, or help out with a home-repair project.

We have a miniature horse named Prince and a small quarter horse named Buck. When my five-year-old twin nieces and eight-year-old nephew visit, I tell them how much Prince and Buck need riding. I tell the kids that we spend so much time with the larger horses, the little ones sometimes get neglected. The kids feel very useful riding and caring for the two smaller horses.

—Ernie Porter, conference center manager

Teach Your Valued Skills

Teach your children skills that are important to you. If you enjoy public speaking, cooking, woodworking, sewing, or sports, take time to impart these skills to your kids.

I taught our children how to use their voices like musical instruments when answering the phone. The kids can now choose from a variety of voices to make themselves sound friendly in unusual ways. They frequently receive compliments from callers on the way they answer the phone. I believe we must teach our children our own treasure chest of gifts.

—Dottie Walters, international speaker and president, Walters International Speakers Bureau

Standing Ovation

The next time your children come to breakfast, give them a standing ovation complete with stomping feet and thunderous applause. Tell them they deserve a standing ovation simply because they're wonderful sons and daughters. Their smiles and gratitude will more than make up for any embarrassment you might feel.

Our family loves Broadway musicals. One Saturday morning after we had taken a trip to New York to see several musicals, my husband and I gave Sondra a standing ovation as she came downstairs for breakfast. We clapped, whistled, and stood on our chairs. Then we proceeded to announce all her wonderful qualities. She loved it.

—Silvana, mother of two girls

Professional Treatment

Sit down with your children and select one or more of their inspiring art pieces. Take the paintings or drawings to a frame shop and have them professionally matted and framed. Tell the framer how proud you are to have such talented kids. Your children will beam, and you'll be guaranteed a lifetime supply of paintings and drawings.

Once a year I select one piece of art from each of my sons and have the works professionally framed. We have an entire wall in our house devoted to these framed pieces. The wall is a chronological museum displaying their development as artists. When relatives and friends visit, they always comment on my children's art.

—Mother of two boys

Teach Kids to Appreciate Others

People have different abilities, and we all deserve proper recognition for the skills and qualities we possess. Help your children learn to appreciate other people's gifts. Children strengthen their character and self-esteem by looking beyond themselves and appreciating how talented and different we all are.

During one four-year period, my husband played basketball in an over-the-hill "slow break" league. My daughter and I were usually the only ones cheering from the bleachers (even though we didn't see many spectacular moves from that motley crew). As a family, we felt since we always attended Trina's games, it made sense for her to reciprocate by going to her dad's games.

—Silvana, mother of two girls

Take Your Child to Work

Expose your children to your professional life. You could have them visit your office or maybe go along on a business trip. Ask your children for advice on how to handle a grumpy coworker or have them help you with simple office tasks. They'll feel important helping you do your job.

My mom took me to work and introduced me to her coworkers as her youngest daughter. Everyone there now knows my name and hobbies (and they probably know how often I get into trouble). It was great knowing that my mom thought of me during the day. We became closer because of that experience.

—J. Harris, student, Central Washington University

Let Kids Decorate Their Bedrooms

Martha Stewart's parents brought her up with "a hammer in one hand and a needle in the other." Her parents encouraged her to decorate her room according to her own taste; the only catch was she had to make whatever she needed. Why not encourage your children to do the same? Teach them how to use fabric paint when decorating plain curtains, or show them how to frame a favorite drawing. They'll feel proud of their accomplishments and more personally attached to their special room.

Even though it was sometimes hard to tolerate, I let my children choose the color schemes and overall themes of their bedrooms. I must admit they got pretty creative!

—*Mother who enjoys plain white walls*

Broaden Kids' Cultural Horizons

Traveling is an eye-opening experience for children. If you live in a house in the suburbs, occasionally visit a city or small rural town. Pay attention to different accents and sample ethnic foods. Even short trips can expose your children to interesting cultures and new environments.

We took our daughter Stephanie and our son Thomas on a trip around the country. We traveled from New Jersey to Houston to Wyoming to Pennsylvania visiting famous historical and geological sites. We spent a month together as a family, and our kids saw many things their friends may never see.

—Steve and Kathy Baumann, state trooper and retail salesperson

Carpe Diem

Demonstrate to your children the exhilaration of seizing the moment. Show them how to be spontaneous and to take advantage of opportunities. Encourage them to take a thought and put it into action, so they won't ever find themselves saying "I wish I had done...."

After my daughter Carrie left for school one day, I realized our chicken eggs were about to hatch. I placed them in a box and brought them to her second-grade class with a lamp to keep them warm. The kids each held a pulsating egg, listened to the scratching inside, and witnessed a new chick coming out. My daughter felt proud to have shared a spontaneous, hands-on experience with her classmates.

—*Maxine Clark, third-grade teacher*

Photo Chronicles

Take pictures of your children on a regular basis and be sure to capture everyday events. In years to come, your kids will enjoy looking back at themselves riding bikes, playing with blocks, and swinging on the swing set.

Our family likes to go out and do fun things like hike and go for ice cream. I always bring along a camera because the kids enjoy having their pictures taken. I like organizing the photos into individual albums so the kids can look back and see how they've grown. The pictures often inspire wonderful stories. I think these albums make them feel very loved.

—Anne Hotchkiss, mother of four and homemaker

Connect with Your Kids

Children experience the world with a light-hearted attitude. Play along with them and laugh at their silly jokes. Pretend you don't know the whoopee cushion is on your seat. Smile as they tell you about their day's events and make direct eye contact whenever possible.

In working with young offenders, two indicators of self-esteem are frequently missing: direct eye contact and smiling. I try to look at my children and smile at them as often as I can.

—*Tom Lagana, coauthor of* Chicken Soup for the Prisoner's Soul

Go the Extra Mile

Go out of your way to make your children feel special. Yes, it's time-consuming to find that special pair of red striped socks they want. Yes, you may have to give up your newspaper time because your son wants help training for a school track meet. Whenever you make that extra effort, try keeping it to yourself.

When my daughter went in for her painful leukemia treatments, she was allowed to pick a small toy from a trinket box after every procedure. I would buy special toys that I knew she wanted and slip them in the box right before it was her turn to choose.

—*Nancy Keene, author*

Respect Your Children's Opinions

It's normal for parents to want specific things for their kids. Parents might have high hopes for an athletic, outgoing, and musical child, while that child is content to be studious and artistic. Encourage your children to try new activities, but make sure to honor their basic personalities and opinions.

My parents came to get me at camp because I refused to eat hot dogs and sloppy joes. The counselors in Omaha didn't understand my vegetarian ways. I'd been a vegetarian almost all my life. My parents ate meat, but they also supported my decision not to eat meat, which was definitely not cool in a town of steak houses!

—*Gail Howerton, professional speaker*

Look Through Your Children's Eyes

Keep your children's perspective in mind. They will often surprise you by enjoying the shiny ribbon more than the expensive gift. To your kids, dinner eaten from play dishes may be more memorable than dining in a fancy restaurant.

My husband and I haven't owned a TV set in over fourteen years. We've spent hours reading and playing with our children. We've gardened, traveled, and built things together. Despite having done all these wonderful activities with our kids, my five-year-old told me the other day that the thing she enjoys most is sleeping in our bed!

—Dr. Barb Brock, professor, Central Washington University

Gifts from the Heart

Take time to acknowledge your children's homemade, heartfelt gifts. The rock covered with tiny pieces of tape represents your child's love for you. The picture dripping with paint means your child thought about adding all your favorite colors to her masterpiece. Even if you're not sure what the gift is, make appreciative comments about the color, shape, or size.

I display the wonderful flowers my children bring me in a vase on the table. We've had wildflowers, dandelions, various weeds, and plants. I usually knock the clods of dirt off first, though.

—Betty Jane Totreault, homeschooling mom

Consequences

As your children get older, allow them to experience the consequences of their actions. Eventually, your kids will appreciate the correlation between actions and the results of those actions. When your children study hard for a test, the natural consequence will usually be a good grade. On the other hand, when they wait until the last minute to do a school project, the result will typically be a low-quality effort.

I was thrilled to get a large part in the junior-high play. The director gave us exactly three weeks to learn our lines. My mom gently reminded me twice to memorize my lines, then she kept quiet. Sure enough, I goofed around, never learned my lines, and lost my part to another student. I was a very quick study in every role after that.

—Drama major and fledgling playwright

Dress Up for Special Events

If your children are involved in a dance recital or formal school event, make the effort to wear something nice. You don't need to wear a gown, just something besides jeans or sweat pants. Your children will notice that you took the time to look nice for their event.

We live in a very casual-dress area. Almost everyone wears jeans to special school events. I try to wear khakis and a nice sweater. I tell my children they're worth it. If one of them has the lead in the play, I even wear lipstick!

—Casual, work-at-home mom

What's a Little Dirt?

If you're on the neat side, try to understand that children are extremely active and they often make a mess. Provide them with plenty of opportunities to spend their seemingly limitless energy, and try not to be terribly concerned about clean fingernails.

A few summers ago, my three boys and I camped under starry skies while frogs, slugs, and creepy-crawly things slithered over our sleeping bags. They laughed when I couldn't find the outhouse in the dark. (They had hidden the flashlight.) I want my boys to experience a wide range of environments from campgrounds to big cities.

—Ingrid Dosta, instructional assistant

Make the Extra Effort

Some children need more attention than others. Give them the boost they need by making every effort to acknowledge their skills and accomplishments.

I helped raise the self-esteem of my shy, overweight ten-year-old by contacting the local newspaper and telling them about his hobby. He had made several trips to maritime museums, which had inspired him to build small ships using twigs and paper. The newspaper published a photograph of him next to his tiny creations. He was very proud.

—*Sally G. Des Marais, mother, grand-mother, and nursery school director for twenty-six years*

Have Kids Pitch In

Give your children age-appropriate responsibilities. Doing chores and contributing to the family's well-being gives children a sense of worth. Explain to your kids how important it is for each family member to do his or her share of cleaning, cooking, walking the dog, and so on.

When we were young, our family took camping trips in Canada every year. The kids were responsible for certain camping-related duties. I still remember how my parents raved about how well we did our jobs.

—Bob Zippiern, college student

Positive Role Models

Look for ways to introduce your children to healthy role models. Check out various hobby-related events such as a meeting of model-railroad enthusiasts or a stamp-and-coin show. People love to talk about their hobbies, and your children benefit from exposure to wholesome activities.

My son, Joe Seale, was born in 1950, when it wasn't easy being a black person in America. His teachers and I knew he was bright, but he needed a successful black role model. Ralph Bunche, former ambassador to the United Nations, was that man. Joe's friends told him things like "Colored boys can't get a job like that." But Joe would say, "I'm going to be like Ralph Bunche. He did it, and so can I." Joe recently graduated from Cornell University.

—proud mother in Florida

Understand Child Development

Educate yourself about behavior that normally occurs at certain ages. If you're aware that toddlers throw tantrums and that teenagers worry about peer pressure, you'll be better able to provide the encouragement and support your children need to develop healthy self-esteem.

I was a typical teenager who didn't want my friends to see me with my parents. To help me through this stage, my parents occasionally took me on spur-of-the-moment trips. They picked me up at school with my luggage already packed, and we traveled to neighboring towns or took long trips back home to Indiana. My parents made sure that we spent time together, and I learned not to be ashamed of my family.

—James McClure, college student

Laugh a Little

Let your children see your sense of humor. Laughter is a great way to relieve stress. Show your kids it's okay to skip down the street or to play a harmless practical joke. We're often so concerned about rules and discipline that we forget to have fun.

As our daughter was preparing to leave for her first day of work at a local deli, she said, "Dad, I don't want to see you spying on me!" Naturally, my wife and I dressed in outlandish outfits that included baggy clothes, fluorescent wigs, and huge glasses. We went to the deli and pretended not to know her. She still talks about how that helped break the ice with her new coworkers.

—Allan, father of two girls

Take Time Out for Togetherness

Tea Party

Enjoy a spontaneous tea party with your children on a rainy Saturday afternoon. Cheer each other up with an afternoon snack complete with candles and china teacups. The formal touches will show your children they deserve a special treat.

I remember how I loved having tea parties with my mother when I was a little girl. My ten-year-old son, however, thinks tea parties are for "sissies." Despite his reluctance, I occasionally set the table with good dishes and pretty flowers. As long as I cut the bread into circles and call them "soccer sandwiches," my son sits with me and enjoys our modified tea party.

—Soccer mom in Seattle

Hang Out with Your Kids

Arrange to have unstructured time with your children in which you simply hang out together. Nothing beats a cup of hot chocolate while reading the comics. Your children will remember the Saturday mornings when everyone stayed in their pajamas playing Monopoly until noon. There's a special closeness that develops when families enjoy time together without a planned agenda.

I learned a big lesson one day when I was putting my seven-year-old to bed. I asked him, "What was the best part of your day?" He told me he really enjoyed helping me barbecue. All we did was sit next to the grill and talk, but it made a big impact on him.

—Dad and teacher

Cherish Ordinary Moments

Let your children know you enjoy their company, even when you're doing routine things. You'd be surprised at how often small opportunities arise when you can say something like "Going to the grocery store is more fun when you come with me." A weekly newspaper once asked fifteen hundred children "What makes a family happy?" The number-one response was "Doing things together."

My daughter and son love dancing with me in the kitchen. We listen to music while cooking dinner. When there's a break in the cooking, we often dance around the table.

—Justin Mitchell, social administrator

Simple Diversions

There comes a time when your children need to break up the routine. Set aside a weekend to get away from it all. You don't need to spend a lot of money, just turn off the TV, unplug the phone, and watch what happens.

We couldn't afford a weekend in a hotel, so we exchanged homes with friends across town. Even though we live only twelve miles apart, our friend's home seemed like a different world. Walking around their neighborhood was really fun. Each family agreed to let answering machines take calls. We relaxed and enjoyed being together on our minivacation.

—Mother and bank teller

Family Lunch at School

Arrange your schedule so you can occasionally have lunch with your children at school. Younger kids love it when parents sit by them in the cafeteria. Older children might prefer a quick trip to McDonald's. Either way, your children will get the message that you enjoy being with them.

I used to pick up my daughter from school three or four times a year. We'd go to a nearby fast food restaurant and enjoy lunch together. One day as I was dropping her off, I overheard her friend say, "Gee, Rachel, your dad must love you an awful lot to take you out to lunch when it's not your birthday."

—Father and engineer

One-on-One Time

One-on-one time between a parent and child is always special. Set up a schedule so your children can anticipate their valued time with you. Write down the special time, if necessary, to help you remember.

I host a "girls' night out" with my daughters. We do things like go to dinner, get ice cream, go window-shopping, and so on. We don't always spend money, but we always have fun. It's a wonderful bonding time.

—Susan Leaf, mother and heiress-wanna-be

Share Discoveries

Share spontaneous discoveries with your children. Have them come outside with you to see the first crocus appearing through the mud. Show them how you repaired the rip in the wallpaper. Let them walk in the rain after a dry spell. Every day presents an opportunity to open your children's eyes to interesting things about the world.

I like to share "discovery moments" with my children. These times can be as simple as seeing a frog on the lawn or noticing a pretty stamp on the envelope from Grandma. I like to talk to them about what we discover. I encourage my children to appreciate the small, pleasant experiences of daily life.

—Dr. Barb Brock, professor, Central Washington University

Silly Traditions

Why not start some silly traditions in your family? I know a family who likes to howl like wolves whenever there's a full moon. Another family has a large garden, and they celebrate "Sneak Zucchini onto Your Neighbor's Porch Day" on August 8. Simple, lighthearted traditions help foster a sense of family togetherness and promote self-esteem in your children.

Whenever a child does a good deed at our summer camp, everyone sings "Skip around the Room." Every kid loves to be chosen to skip around the room. Campers are rewarded for their good behavior, and big smiles always follow.

—Kathy Baumann, board of directors, Camp Ma-he-tu

"Special Week" Calendar

Every month, give your children a seven-day calendar that contains an activity for each day of the special week. On Monday, you might ride bikes to the park. On Tuesday, you might do a craft project. On Wednesday, you might assemble a puzzle. The activities don't have to take much time or money, and your children will always appreciate your undivided attention during their special week.

About fifteen minutes before I start dinner, my kids and I check the "Low-Key Activity Calendar." I take turns with the girls doing a short, fun activity that we've already planned. It's convenient to look at the calendar and read "Mom and Gabby rearrange stuffed animals." The calendar eliminates the pressure to come up with things to do.

—Mother and graphic designer

Special Time Together

Show your children you enjoy playing with them. Whenever time allows, add a few minutes of fun while you're completing errands or chores.

Every year, my children spend "special time" with me while we shop for back-to-school clothes. They carry their own money, and they're allowed to make major decisions about what to buy. We have great conversations and enjoy each other's undivided attention. We always include lunch at their favorite restaurant.

—*Darlene VanderYacht, paraprofessional*

Volunteer as a Family

Find ways to volunteer as a family. Special Olympics teams frequently need help, and your local Humane Society always needs volunteers to walk dogs. Your children will learn important lessons by helping others, and the supportive feedback will further boost their self-confidence.

With four children, it's sometimes difficult to volunteer as a family. My nine-year-old came up with the idea of making "bedtime snack sacks" for needy children. Once a month, I set ten paper lunch bags on a table. The younger children decorate them with crayons and glitter. The older children fill the sacks with juice, granola bars, fruit leather, and a small toy. Then, as a family, we deliver the bags to a homeless shelter.

—Leslie Johnson, mother of four

Undivided Attention

One of the most effective ways to make your children feel special is to give them your undivided attention. Even if you're rushed, say something like "I'm going to sit here while you tell me about the fort you built because I want to hear all about it. Then I need to go back and make dinner."

I've filled a void in my stepdaughter's life by allowing her to talk about issues she's not comfortable discussing with her parents. I give her the freedom to ask me whatever she wants. In return, I'm allowed to ask her important questions. This makes her feel comfortable and mature.

—Kimberly Raymer, author

Car-Trip Fun

On long car trips, have one child sit up front and have a parent take a back seat. If you have only one adult in the car, rotate the children so they get equal time up front. By separating siblings, you'll find there's less bickering. Plus, parents get to talk individually with children. The entire atmosphere changes. Make sure the kids who sit up front are old enough for air-bag safety.

Out of habit, my husband gets behind the wheel for long trips. Last year, I suggested a change. I was tired of monitoring back-seat squabbles, so I asked him to sit in the back while I drove. He happily played alphabet bingo with our eight-year-old while I sat up front with my teenage daughter. The two of us enjoyed wonderful, uninterrupted conversation. She talked the entire trip!

—Stay-at-home mom

Family Outfits

Teenagers might roll their eyes mockingly, but younger children enjoy dressing like Mom or Dad. One family decorated plain-colored T-shirts with fabric paint to wear to a family reunion. If your older kids don't want to be seen in public looking like the Von Trapp family singers, make or buy family T-shirts that double as night shirts.

My husband and three sons took a "guys only" trip one year. I had hats made with "Thoma Guys" embroidered on the front, which they wore proudly.

—*Sandy Thoma, marriage-and-family therapist*

Keep Close When You're Apart

The Next Best Thing

If you're going away for a few days, tape-record a loving message for your child and leave it on his pillow. Describe where you are and what you're doing, tell him a favorite bedtime story, and send a special good-night kiss. You might also sing a familiar song, especially one that's part of your bedtime routine.

In a strange way, my kids actually looked forward to my business trips. They enjoyed the tapes I left for them. In addition to telling them a story, I'd say something like "Before you close your eyes, check your sock drawer for a special treat." They'd find a small trinket or a coupon for an ice-cream cone.

—Traveling dad in Boston

Holiday Gifts

If you're separated from your children on a holiday, use the mail service to stay connected. Send small St. Patrick's Day earrings, Halloween candy, or New Year's confetti. Lightweight items cost very little to mail, and they go a long way toward making children feel special. Some parents mail presents as they're leaving town, to make sure gifts arrive on time.

Every spring, I send Easter baskets wrapped in a padded bag envelope to my kids at college. I'll use almost any excuse to send them something special to remind them how important they are to our family.

—Stephanie Siemens, camp director and author

Camp Connections

Look for ways to keep in touch with your children when they're away at residential camp or spending a week at Grandma's. Tuck brief notes in their pockets or wrap new pajamas for them to wear on their first night away from home. One mother taped a goofy picture of herself on the inside of her son's suitcase. (He promptly removed it to avoid embarrassment.)

As my daughters prepare to attend resident Girl Scout camp, we gather as a group to pack the belongings they'll need. Each day's clothes are packed in individual Ziploc bags that include a loving note of encouragement.

—Donna Winders, director of program services

Send Videotapes to Your Relatives

Keep in touch with distant relatives by mailing videotapes of your children's energetic capers. Document daily activities such as playing the piano and jumping on the trampoline. Grandparents love watching these stirring documentaries, and your kids will enjoy being the center of attention.

My children had never met my sister's children, and we wanted the cousins to get acquainted prior to an upcoming reunion. So, my sister and I each video-taped our kids doing everyday activities such as playing in the yard, wrestling, and brushing teeth. The kids loved watching their cousins. Most importantly, the children felt like friends when they finally met.

—Teacher and mother of three

Fax a Message or Picture

If you're out of town and you have a fax machine at home, draw a silly picture or write a loving note and fax it to your children. Some parents fax messages to their kids at school. Your children will enjoy getting a note reading "Jason, good luck on your history test. I love you. Dad."

When Sondra was four, she drew a simple, charming picture of a dog. We decided to fax it to Grandma. To our surprise, Grandma faxed the picture back after adding some flowers and a cat. Sondra then drew a doghouse and faxed it back to Grandma. The picture just grew and grew. Thank goodness it was a local call!

—*Silvana, mother of two girls*

Family Newsletter

Help your children stay in touch with relatives by publishing a family newsletter. You could create a two-page flier or a twenty-page document complete with color photos. The newsletter will help keep your kids posted on what's happening in other families, and it will help your children remain close to extended family members who live far away.

Our family publishes its newsletter every couple of months. We use a simple template and invite family members to plug in stories everyone will appreciate such as Sarah losing her first tooth, Mom running a 5K race, Fluffy having three kittens, and so on. We keep copies in a three-ring binder, and everyone enjoys reviewing past issues.

—Landscaper and mother of two

Family Cookbook

A wonderful way to strengthen family ties and nurture your children's self-esteem is to make a family recipe book. Have all family members, including distant relatives, submit their favorite recipes. Ask them to include anecdotes, too. Assemble the books using simple bindings and copy machines, or have a local printer help out. Your children will enjoy drawing illustrations.

We invited our extended family to submit recipes for a family cookbook. It was fun reading about "Alison's Absolutely Scrumptious Scrambled Eggs." The family grew closer even though most of us lived thousands of miles apart. The kids felt proud to be published authors.

—Mother and cookbook creator

Camp Mail

Children enjoy the special thrill of getting mail at residential camp. But woe to the camper who receives an envelope covered with lipstick or drenched in perfume! Send the first letter to your children two to three days before they leave for camp. That way they'll get mail on the first day.

While our daughter was at camp, my husband sent several postcards containing mushy messages and "phony" signatures. Naturally, these letters were read aloud to the entire camp. Our daughter acted embarrassed, but we know she loved it.

—Mother and dental hygienist

Creative Postcards

Communicate with your children when you're out of town through the creative use of postcards. Show your kids you think they're special by sending each one a postcard. Here's the catch: Your children have to lay out the postcards side by side in order to read the complete message. If you have only one child, send several postcards and have her fit them together to read the message.

I keep a variety of generic postcards for surprise business trips. I mail one to my kids from home the day before I leave town. That way my children get a postcard the day I'm gone. They have yet to notice the local postmark.

—Dad and consultant

Let Your Kids Help You Pack

If you're leaving home for a few days, have your children help you prepare for the trip. Ask them to suggest reading material to take along. If you're lucky, your youngsters might draw pictures to put in your suitcase. You could show your kids the nonbreakable frames you carry that contain their photographs. You could also explain how you display the pictures in your hotel room as soon as you arrive.

When I was younger, my parents occasionally went to dinner with their friends on Friday night. My mom let me choose her outfit—dress, shoes, jewelry, everything— and she actually wore what I chose!

—Kelly Redfield, college student

"I Miss You"

Tell your children how much you miss them when you're away. Explain how you visualize what they're doing while you're gone.

My wife and I periodically take business trips. Before we leave, we remind our children that the reason we miss them so much is because we love them. Recently, I was preparing to leave on a trip, and I was telling my five-year-old how much I would miss her. She reminded me that it was okay, because missing her meant that I really loved her. I sometimes think she gets it better than I do.

—Robert MacPhee, proud dad

Travel Routines

Develop a routine for your children that takes place whenever you leave home for a while. Give your kids a copy of your flight itinerary and hotel phone number. Explain to them what you'll be doing on the trip. Children often assume that you're taking a vacation and don't realize you have work to do. Routines help your children stay connected to you while your hectic life pulls you away.

When I'm out of town, I call my children in the morning while they're getting ready for school. Sometimes I have to get up early when I'm in a different time zone, but the day doesn't start right until I connect with my family.

—Dad and computer consultant

Give the Ultimate Gift: Your Time

If you travel often, try to avoid the "I'll bring you back a toy" routine. Your children will start to look forward to their gifts more than to your return. Instead, promise to play basketball or ride bikes with them when you get back. Your time is the most precious gift you can give.

When my wife needed to leave home on speaking engagements, Sondra and I would carefully select what costumes to wear when we picked her up at the airport. We dressed as Dorothy and the Scarecrow, Peter Pan and Captain Hook, and even Christine and the Phantom of the Opera. We did this for two years until we ran out of costume ideas!

—Allan, father of two girls

Explain Your Family Tree

Explain to your children how they fit into their extended family. If reunions don't occur often, encourage your children to use e-mail or regular letters to keep in touch with their relatives. Kids develop a special sense of security knowing they have cousins, aunts, uncles, and grandparents who love and care for them.

I designed a book for my children that contained photographs of our relatives. We kept the book by the phone so that when a cousin called, we flipped to the page with the cousin's face on it. This helped remind the kids of the person they were talking to, and this also helped the kids develop a deeper bond with family members far away.

—Artist and mother of three

Special "Welcome Home" Greeting

Establish a special greeting for family members who've been away from home. For example, if your children are returning home from a week at camp or from visiting Grandma, let them know you're glad to see them with a special family greeting.

In our family, whenever someone is away from home for more than two nights, we place an electric candle in the window by the front door. We keep the candle "burning" twenty-four hours a day, so that even if family members return during the day, the candle is there to greet them. Our daughter came home from college a few months ago and was disappointed because we'd forgotten to plug in the candle for her!

—Dad and mechanic

Lunch Notes

Use your children's lunch bags to communicate loving sentiments. Write notes on their napkins or include surprise messages in their lunches. One mother used tweezers to remove the paper fortunes from fortune cookies. Then, she painstakingly replaced the papers with personalized fortunes for her kids. (Yes, I know it's a bit extreme!)

Part of my parental responsibility at home involves packing our children's lunches. I always include "Daddy's Special Surprise." This might be a Tootsie Roll, a new eraser, or whatever comes to mind. The kids look forward to their surprises and show them to friends and teachers.

—Rich Garbinsky, camp director

Express Your Love with Words and Art

Birth Letter

Soon after your child is born, write her a letter describing the impact she had on your family. Share your feelings about the wonders of pregnancy, describe how you decorated the nursery, tell the delivery story (you might want to avoid any agonizing details), explain how her siblings were preparing for the new baby, and so on. Give your child the letter around her tenth birthday, so she'll be better able to appreciate the powerful emotions you were feeling.

Even though I was exhausted, I wrote a letter to my son the day after he was born. I knew he probably wouldn't appreciate it until he had children of his own, but I wanted to convey to him the overwhelming sense of love I had for him the instant he was born.

—Mother and nurse

Design a Family Tree

Help your children understand their heritage by making a family tree together. You could use simple line drawings with names, or you could include photographs and sketches. Even if you list only two or three generations, the family tree will further instill a sense of belonging in your kids. The tree will also remind them of family members beyond their immediate world.

Our first son, Christopher, became "big brother" after the birth of our second son, Michael. Chris struggled with the change for a while. Sometimes he would shout, "I'm nobody!" We would remind him of his cousins in Texas, his uncles in Fresno and San Francisco, and the rest of his extended family. Chris eventually realized he was still Christopher—our son who had a big family to introduce his little brother to.

—Steve Shively, conference center director

School Mail

Try writing a letter to your child and mailing it to him at school. Remember how exciting it felt when a messenger walked into the classroom and handed the teacher a note for someone? The room was filled with anxious eyes waiting to see who would be the lucky recipient. Unless your child is extremely shy, he'll enjoy the surprise of getting an unexpected letter from you at school.

I always sent birthday cards to my children at school. My kids got a big kick out of receiving brightly colored cards from the messengers. The cards actually made a bigger impact than if I had handed them to my kids with their presents.

—Father of two preteens

Personal Posters

Give your children a large piece of colored poster board so they can create personalized posters. Supply magazines and photos to help them make a collage of the activities they enjoy. Encourage your kids to leave space for adding pictures as new interests develop. Display the collages in a prominent location in your home.

I have two wonderful daughters ages six and seven. We keep posters next to their beds where they draw or paste pictures of things they're good at or want to be good at. We call the posters "I Am Super Good!"

—*Hank DeFelice, professional speaker*

Secret Pal

Designate yourself a "secret pal" to your children. Hide small gifts in their rooms or put secret messages in their gym bags. Eventually your kids will suspect the notes are from you, but they'll still enjoy the attention. Also, consider exchanging names within your family and have everyone do something nice for their designated person.

When my children were young, I would secretly admire them by sending cards signed "Secret Pal." I wouldn't reveal my identity unless it was absolutely necessary. When I mailed the cards, I'd write a different return address on the envelope to conceal my identity. They enjoyed the special attention.

—*Rhonda Lennon, medical receptionist and Tupperware manager*

Birthday Newspaper

It's never too late to begin saving the news-papers from your children's birthdays. They'll enjoy looking back and reading about what was happening in the world on their special days.

My mother-in-law gave me a copy of the newspaper from the day my daughter was born. I enjoyed reading that paper so much I saved my daughter's birthday papers for the next nine years. Even now, she likes looking at the ads from years ago and noticing how fashions have changed. I was much busier with my son, so he has a few years missing!

—Mother and writer

Discuss Famous Quotations with Your Kids

Expose your children to a wide variety of thoughts by reading quotations from different cultures and historical periods. Ask your kids what they think the statements mean.

I love quotes. I often prepared a whole sheet of them for our dinner table. I'd read one and ask my kids to guess the year, author, important events of the time, and how the meaning might apply to our own lives. We introduced our children to the great conversation of humanity. One of their favorite quotes was by Confucius' teacher, Leo Tsze: "To see things in the seed—that is genius."

—Dottie Walters, international speaker and president, Walters International Speakers Bureau

Screen Saver

Use your computer's screen saver to convey words and images of encouragement to your children. Import photographs of your kids as background wallpaper, or write a loving message on the scrolling screen saver. If you don't know how to do this, ask your children to demonstrate—they'll be delighted to show off their computer skills.

I use the scrolling message screen saver on our computer to send special notes to my son including "Great report card!" "Happy birthday!" "Number-one soccer player!" "I love you!" and so on. He looks forward to seeing new messages as I change them.

—Marie Meador, director, 4-H Center

Personal Notebook

Provide special notebooks for your children in which they can write notes and draw pictures about daily events. After your kids are grown, they'll enjoy looking back and seeing how their handwriting improved and how their artistic skills increased. Some families incorporate journals into bedtime routines.

During the time my husband is commercial fishing in Alaska, communication is limited to scratchy phone calls. So, the kids and I keep daily journals of our summer activities. When my husband comes home, we pick a date and everyone reads what happened that day. The journals help keep us connected as a family. We relive the summer's experiences and show my husband how much we were thinking about him while he was gone.

—Mother of three children

Messages on Toast

Send fun messages to your children using toast as a canvas! Pour one tablespoon of evaporated milk into each of three bowls. Add a few drops of food coloring to each bowl and stir. (Select a different color for each bowl.) Use a clean paintbrush to paint a picture or write a short message on the bread. Put the bread in the toaster and watch your children's faces brighten when they see the design!

It's difficult to get my children motivated for school on Monday mornings during gloomy winter months. To counteract the winter blues, we have a tradition where, every Monday, I write messages on their toast and cut it into fancy shapes using cookie cutters.

—*Mother and librarian*

Teach Your Kids to Send Letters

The convenience of e-mail is hard to ignore, but also introduce your children to letter writing as a method of keeping in touch with distant family members. Start your kids out with letters to grandparents because they tend to respond quickly and enthusiastically. Your children will enjoy the excitement of going to the mailbox and finding letters addressed to them!

My children love to receive mail. Every so often, they sit down and draw pictures on blank postcards and send them to friends and family. After a week or so, my five- and seven-year-old get mail personally addressed to them.

—Elizabeth Donnenwirth, illustrator

Do Homework Together

Instead of sending your children to their rooms to do homework, have them sit with you at the kitchen table or in the living room. (Make sure the TV is turned off.) You can balance your checkbook or read quietly while they do math or social studies. They'll see you actively involved in your own homework projects, and you'll be close by when they need a little help.

My two children sit at the dinner table to do their homework. My husband and I spend time sitting next to them, usually reading. After fifteen minutes or so, we leave, but by then the kids have settled into their routine and are concentrating on their studies.

—Self-employed mother

Have Kids Write Their Own Books

Children, especially beginning or reluctant readers, enjoy reading books about themselves. Encourage your kids to write stories about their lives. Have them look at a few personal photographs and begin telling a story. Write down their words or tape-record the narration and write it down later. Use the photographs for illustrations. Your kids will feel proud to have written their own books.

Once a year, I choose a special day to take pictures of my son. I photograph him playing with the dog, brushing his teeth, riding his bike, and so on. We use the pictures to make a book called "Jordan's Busy Day." We now have six "Busy Day" books. It's fun to look back and see how his daily activities have changed throughout the years.

—Mother and teacher

Family Bulletin Board

Help your children create a "family appreciation" bulletin board. Buy a bulletin board or designate a section of the refrigerator as the message board for family members. Parents will probably write most of the notes, but don't be surprised to find an occasional message from one sibling to another. Have a rule that all notes must be positive. The praise and attention your kids receive will further boost their self-esteem.

I bought a red bulletin board and hung it in the family room. My husband and I started writing notes like "Check out the bird feeder. Melissa did a great job cleaning and refilling it." Our kids loved the public acknowledgement of their efforts.

—Mom and piano teacher

Wearable Art

Here's a great way to preserve and publicize your children's drawings and notes. Gather your cherished pieces and have a quick-print shop transfer them to photo transfer paper. You can create T-shirts or quilts by ironing the transfer onto light-colored fabric. Your kids will love seeing their artwork displayed on the front of your shirt.

I recently looked through my kids' childhood drawings and selected my favorite paintings and flat artwork. I then used these pieces to make unique quilts for my two older children.

—Michal Handy, school bus driver

Document Your Kids' Development

Document your children's progress as they're learning new skills. When they're older, they'll see how they first printed their names or first wrote in cursive. Ask your kids to draw yearly self-portraits so you can catalog their artistic development, too.

We photographed our daughters while they cooked and used the pictures as covers for the girls' individual cookbooks. Each time one learned a new recipe, we added it to her cookbook. By the time the girls left for college, each had an impressive collection of tried-and-true recipes. It was fun to notice how the recipes increased in sophistication, from their first scrambled eggs to decadent cheesecakes.

—Laurie Keleman, former teacher

Creative Praise

Be creative when acknowledging your children's accomplishments. Instead of always giving them stickers or happy faces, look for unique ways to highlight their successes.

Every summer, we transform a wall in our house into the "reading wall." Last year, we drew a tree on the wall and the kids painted leaves on the tree for every book they read. This summer, we transformed the wall into a sky and the kids drew kites, birds, and airplanes for every book they read. Every week or two during the summer, I take pictures of the kids standing against the wall, so that when summer's over, they can see what they accomplished. They've become great readers.

—Kathy Moreno, stay-at-home mother of three children

Qualities List

We make lists for everything—groceries, toiletries, errands, and so on. Why not list the wonderful qualities your children demonstrate every day? Once a week or so, have your children consult the list to remind themselves how amazing they are.

We helped our son make a list of fifty things he liked about himself. We encouraged him to focus on personal qualities rather than accomplishments. By doing this, he learned his self-worth came from within. We tried to remind him every day of the wonderful qualities he possessed.

—Ed Kania, CPA, director of business services

Celebrity Autographs

Try to obtain autographs from your children's favorite sports heroes or celebrities. Many children's book authors reply favorably to autograph requests. Search the Internet for celebrity addresses and autograph opportunities. Include a self-addressed stamped envelope for a quick reply.

When Trina was ten, she wanted to star in Annie *on Broadway. She walked around the house singing "Tomorrow" constantly. I wrote to the young girl who was playing Annie on Broadway at the time, and she sent Trina two personalized Christmas cards and a short note. Those cards were the highlight of Trina's Christmas that year.*

—Silvana, mother of two girls

Share Your Children's News

Spread the word to friends and family about your children's impressive academic accomplishments and artistic masterpieces. Wrap Grandma's birthday present using your preschooler's finger-painted pictures. Make greeting cards using your children's watercolor paintings, or write letters to family on the backs of your kids' spelling tests. Everyone will enjoy the personalized attention, especially your children.

My eight-year-old daughter Alison loves to write. A while ago, I collected some of her favorite pieces and sent them to our distant relatives. She received lots of appreciative comments from her grandparents, aunts, and uncles.

—Nancy Keene, author

Tangible Incentives

Children often need concrete reinforcement reminding them of the steps they've taken toward reaching a goal. Experiment to see what incentive program works best for your children.

Every kid in our family had a chart with fifty footprints on it. Whenever we did something praiseworthy, our parents allowed us to fill in a footprint. When one child reached the fiftieth footprint, he or she got to select our next family activity. We usually picked a movie or bowling or miniature golf. It felt really special picking the family activity.

—Staci Schuerman, college student

Kid Contracts

For important issues like allowance, you might consider drawing up contracts with your children. If they're earning money for camp, list the chores they should do and how much you'll pay for each job. Include incentive programs for earning extra cash or privileges. Specific guidelines give children a clear sense of what is expected.

My daughter wanted a raise in her allowance, so we designed a four-week trial period in which she could complete extra chores and make extra money. The contract outlined her normal duties, the consequences of neglecting those duties, additional chores, and the amounts to be earned. It worked out well and saved me from having to nag her.

—Mother and administrative assistant

E-mail Your Kids

Stay in touch with your children by using e-mail. If you have access to computers and the Internet, it's incredibly easy and fun. Many schools allow children to have their own e-mail accounts. Send simple greetings or use one of the free cards available off the Internet. Even reluctant letter writers tend to enjoy e-mail.

I send e-mail to my daughters at school. It's a great way to say "Hi" and to let them know I'm thinking of them. I especially love getting their responses!

—Teri Bodensteiner, registered nurse

Write Notes to Your Children

Writing notes and letters to your children is a great way to communicate your love. Your kids can reread the messages several times. You might even find them stashing your notes in a drawer and taking them out periodically to look at. Letters are still a great way to say "I love you."

When I returned to work full-time, I started the habit of sending special notes to my boys in their lunch bags three times a week. My oldest is thirteen, and he loves them, although he doesn't read them to his friends. However, I discovered that his friends have asked their moms to write notes, too.

—Barbara Davidson, superintendent of recreation

Confront Challenges with Courage

Provide Concrete Learning Strategies

Facilitate your children's learning by providing practical tips when they're struggling to acquire new skills. For example, you might say to your child "Learning all these lines for the play takes serious time. Would you like me to help you rehearse after dinner? Sometimes it's easier to memorize lines if someone speaks the cue lines." Children often feel overwhelmed by new and complex tasks, so help out by teaching them effective ways to learn.

My son was getting frustrated with toilet training, so I wadded up a ball of toilet paper, threw it in the toilet, and told him, "Aim and hit it." It worked!

—Marilyn Lampman, bus driver

Teach Kids to Think Outside the Box

Teach your children to think creatively when attempting to solve problems or make decisions. Encourage them to search for alternative methods of handling challenging situations.

When my children were little, I'd send them on creative scavenger hunts to find items such as "mouse chairs" or "gnome hats." They ingeniously searched for objects that would help them produce the requested item. There was never a wrong answer, so the game always boosted their self-esteem and helped them solve problems in creative ways.

—Marjorie Crum, graphic designer

A Helping Hand

Sometimes, a little carefully timed help is all children need to keep trying until they succeed. Judiciously choose the timing and amount of intervention based on your children's personalities. Give them enough room to work out their problems, stepping in only when necessary.

My three- and five-year-old sat at their lemonade stand for several hours and only made fifteen cents. So, I gave some older neighborhood kids a dollar to buy lemonade and leave a tip. The older kids felt like big shots and my kids were thrilled to earn a dollar.

—*Elementary school principal*

Encourage Problem Solving

Teach your children to make lemonade out of lemons. Researchers have reported that people who actively seek out solutions to their problems tend to be more optimistic. When your children are faced with unpleasant situations, show them how to avoid complaining and get results instead.

Several years ago, we moved to Oregon to start a new business, and our daughter Carrie had to go to a new school. At the time, we couldn't afford the fancy lunch boxes the other children had, so I drew colorful cartoons on her lunch sacks instead. It wasn't long before her fellow students wanted me to draw on their lunch sacks, too. The new girl fit right in.

—Trish Henifin, school bus driver

Model Healthy Self-Esteem

Demonstrate behavior that reflects your own healthy self-esteem. Take new classes, share books you're reading, tell your kids how you handled a difficult situation with a friend, and so on. Practice what you preach, and your lessons will have an even greater impact on your children.

I frequently remind myself that self-esteem and high self-esteem are not the same thing. I need to have high self-esteem in order to help my children build their own. So, I continually do things that build my self-esteem. It's contagious.

—*Tom Lagana, coauthor of* Chicken Soup for the Prisoner's Soul

Listen First

When your children misbehave or disobey, give them a chance to explain themselves first. Listen closely to what they're saying and use the situation as a learning experience. This will also give you a chance to collect your thoughts and get your emotions under control. Remember, the word discipline means "to teach." Our job as parents is to lovingly teach our children to learn from their mistakes.

I've learned in my personal and professional life that kids need someone who will listen to their side of the story and who will recognize that it is hard to grow up today.

—*Teresa Huggins, parent, teacher, and counselor*

Avoid the Rush

Try to go a full day without saying "Hurry up!" to your children. Teach them to manage their time and accept the consequences of being late. Time management is a valuable life skill that is sometimes best learned the hard way.

I established a routine in which my daughter selected her clothes and organized her backpack every night before school. In the morning, I'd give her one five-minute warning before it was time to leave. When time was up, I'd walk to the car, get inside, and start reading a book. On days she was late, it was her responsibility to explain to the principal why she was tardy. She rose to the challenge well and now monitors her time expertly.

—*Mother and textile designer*

Teach Effective Coping Strategies

Teach your children strategies for handling situations they find stressful. If other kids tease your children on the bus, have them act out several ways of dealing with the negative behavior. For example, have your children memorize phrases to use in difficult situations. This will give them confidence under pressure.

My son was often picked on by an older cousin at family get-togethers. We role-played a few things my son could say when his cousin teased him. At the next Christmas party, the teasing began again. My son made direct eye contact and used one of the statements he had rehearsed. His cousin was so surprised at the forceful response that he left my son alone.

—Nurse and mother of twins

Teach Financial Responsibility

When you think your children are old enough, introduce them to your family's financial situation. Show them how much the electricity, phone, cable, garbage collection, and rent or mortgage cost. Give them money-management experience whenever possible. For example, have them make a shortened grocery list and pay for items without exceeding a designated amount.

When our family went on vacation, we gave each child 150 dollars to spend per day. At first, the kids thought it was a fortune, but they soon realized how quickly hotel, food, souvenirs, and snacks eat up expenses. They became more price conscious after that and kept a running tab of all our costs.

—Penny-pinching parents

Respect Children's Reactions to Death

Honor your children's feelings after the death of a relative, friend, or pet. Children don't mourn the same way adults do because the concept of death is difficult for them to understand.

My children's grandmother passed away on her birthday, and the entire family had a special ceremony in the backyard where we sang "Happy Birthday" and released helium balloons. As the kids watched the balloons fly away, they were convinced they saw their grandmother gathering the balloons. It was a very special event for everybody.

—G. Coldwell, skating-rink owner

Special Treatment

Whenever your children are sick, take the time to provide extraspecial attention. If your kids don't feel like eating solid food, mix up fruit smoothies and serve them in a fancy glass. Provide a small bell for your children to ring if they need anything.

When my daughter Ayla was ill, her dad told her how his mother used to rub Vicks on his chest and feet when he was sick. I searched the house for an hour and a half and finally found a small, half-empty jar of Vicks. After I finished rubbing her chest and massaging her feet, she said, "I'm still cold, I can't breathe, and my head still hurts...but my feet feel so much better. Thanks, Mom!"

—*Gloria Barber, business owner*

Praise Hard Work

Celebrate when your children bring home their report cards. Even if the grades aren't perfect, you can applaud the progress made in certain areas. Emphasize the importance of doing one's best. Straight As come easily for some kids, but other children struggle to get good grades. Praise their efforts as well as their accomplishments.

Whenever our kids brought home their report cards, we went out to a family restaurant that had a make-your-own ice-cream bar. The kids were allowed to eat as much ice cream as they wanted without a parent telling them they'd had enough. If grades needed to be improved, it was discussed at a later time.

—Mother and lab technician

Encourage Independent Behavior

Promoting independent behavior in our children can sometimes be an onerous task. It's often easier for us to help our kids tie their shoes or make their snacks instead of waiting for them to do it themselves. But children need to experience independent accomplishments in order to develop healthy self-esteem.

On certain school days when my seven-year-old is home well before dinner time, I let him make an after-school snack using leftovers from the fridge. I also encourage him to create a name for the snack. Since he makes it, he usually eats all of it.

—Kevin Sullivan, camp director

The Importance of Earning Money

Instead of begrudgingly buying your kids the latest gizmos, have them earn the money. Working, budgeting, and saving for toys teaches kids valuable decision-making skills.

We gave our children paychecks, not allowances. When they wanted to buy something, we said, "Let's figure out how you can earn the money." We taught them fiscal self-reliance, not whining and begging. When Mike was in junior high, he worked as the cleanup boy in our print shop. On his first day, his dad handed him a stopwatch and told him to time each job he completed. Each time he figured out how to do something more efficiently, he got a raise.

—Dottie Walters, international speaker and president, Walters International Speakers Bureau

Invent and Enjoy Special Occasions

Celebrate the New Baby

Whenever a new baby is brought home, family dynamics shift dramatically. If you already have children, invite them to share the joy at this baby's birth that you felt at their births. Talk about the skills and privileges your children have acquired over the years and how much the new baby has to look forward to.

When my third child was born, I had two baskets of flowers delivered to the elementary school my older children attended. I wanted to congratulate them on the birth of their new sister.

—Lori Tomenchok, teacher

Creative Touches

Use creativity when celebrating your children's special occasions. Insert candles into their stack of pancakes. Hide cards in their homework. Write "Happy Birthday" with washable marker on their bathroom mirror.

Our kids really enjoy the family tradition in which we pick them up from school on their birthdays. When we arrive home, they excitedly push the garage door opener to discover that I've attached crepe paper and strings of balloons to the inside-bottom edge of the garage door. They love seeing the colorful signs and decorations appear as the door opens. Then we drive through the cascade of birthday decorations.

—Artist and mother of three children

Birthday Place Mat

Design a birthday place mat for your child by gluing pictures and mementos of the past year onto a colorful piece of cardboard. Include photos, ticket stubs from sporting events or school plays, drawings, and so on. Cover the place mat with clear adhesive paper or have it professionally laminated at a print shop.

I have a special manila envelope for each of my children. I use the envelopes to store funny photographs, report cards, drawings, sketches, ticket stubs, and lots of their other personal items. As one of their birthdays approaches, I use the envelope's contents to make a collage place mat. We now have a wonderful collection of childhood memories in the form of birthday place mats.

—Mother of three boys

Have Kids Plan Birthday Parties

As parents, we often assume the responsibility for planning our children's birthday parties. However, as your kids get older, let them play a larger role in deciding what happens. Give them a few guidelines and provide assistance as needed, but let them make important decisions and generally do as much as they want.

Our daughter Keli helped us plan a "grocery store scavenger hunt" for her birthday. She invited her friends and we gave everyone money for the hunt. The kids bought what they needed for dinner, snacks, and breakfast. They enjoyed the independence of deciding what to buy for their party.

—Sandy Thoma, marriage-and-family therapist

Announce Your Child's Special Events

Use your newspaper's classified ads or society section to announce important events in your children's lives. You can often include a photograph for a small fee. Circle the ad in red and ask your kids to look through the classifieds. They'll be excited to see their names in print. The cost is low, but the impact is high.

About twice a year, we celebrate our son's accomplishments by placing an ad in the newspaper's miscellaneous section. Previous ads have read "Michael, we're proud of your hard work in the math contest" and "Thanks for helping Grandpa build his tool shed." Seeing his efforts recognized in the paper makes him feel special.

—Dad and carpenter

Celebrate Accomplishments

Acknowledge your children's attempts to try new things. Bring out the balloons and streamers when your daughter auditions for the school play. Celebrate when your son's training wheels come off or when your daughter cooks her first scrambled eggs.

I buy balloons and other party supplies at the dollar store. I like to keep a healthy supply of party items on hand to celebrate my son's achievements. We recently celebrated his first attempt at climbing a tree and his successful completion of swimming lessons. We even celebrated when the puppy was housebroken!

—Mother and administrative assistant

Special Plate

Find a distinctive plate for your child to enjoy on special occasions. For example, when she masters multiplication tables or helps a new child at school, she gets to enjoy the privelege of eating off the special plate.

Our family recently visited antique stores looking for a fancy plate. We have a rather twisted sense of humor, so we wound up with a plate that had a roller-skating rooster painted on it. Whenever our kids get a hundred on a spelling test, they get to eat off the rooster plate. We even let Grandpa eat off it once after he got new dentures!

—Mother of three high-spirited children

Birthday Party Options

Provide several options for your children when planning their birthday parties. Children often assume traditional parties are the only way to go. Brainstorm various possibilities such as going to a movie with friends, hosting a birthday breakfast, or enjoying a pool party. One nine-year-old asked her guests to bring canned food for the food bank instead of gifts.

I decided to put a twist on the traditional "Sweet Sixteen" birthday party. My mom helped me plan a "Sour Sixteen" party. The menu included sweet and sour chicken, pickles, chips with sour cream and chives, lemon cake, and lemon sorbet. We had a blast.

—Anya Rose, aspiring scientist

Everyday Family Traditions

Regular activities can become special occasions when unique family traditions are established to highlight the events. Read bedtime stories by flashlight once a week, or bake cinnamon rolls on Saturday mornings while everyone does chores.

Every Saturday morning while my daughter was young, my husband let me sleep in while he enjoyed special time with Brie. They woke up early and walked to McDonald's. Brie got to order her own breakfast, and she also selected a cup of black coffee and a small orange juice for my husband. He gave her the money and let her pay for it. This experience gave her the confidence to speak to strangers and be listened to at a young age.

—Gay Fakkema, operations supervisor

Celebrate the First Day of School

The first day of every school year deserves to be celebrated. The kids are usually excited and the atmosphere is hectic, but try to allow time for a leisurely breakfast. Some parents set the table with fancy china to enhance the festivities. Show your children you value education by putting encouraging notes in their lunch boxes.

Each time one of our kids started kinder-garten, we planted a special tree. On the first day of each school year, we took pic-tures of the kids in front of their special trees. It's fun to look back and see how the children have grown alongside their trees.

—Michal and Frank Hardy, school bus drivers

Encourage Social Activities

Help your children plan events that include other people. Encourage them to share activities with family and friends. You never know when a party might break out—or a new family tradition.

During my children's elementary years, we invited the neighborhood kids to a "snow scene" party every winter. My husband designed up to twenty-five trays from cardboard and aluminum foil. The kids covered their cardboard trays with mounds of "snow" that I whipped up from Ivory Flakes. Then, the kids decorated their "winter" scenes with twigs, pebbles, animal cutouts, and mirrors for ponds. These parties furnished us with many fond memories.

—Maxine Clark, third-grade teacher

Give Experiences as Birthday Gifts

Go all-out to celebrate your child's birthday by giving memorable experiences instead of expensive presents. Balloons at the foot of the bed, birthday cake for breakfast, or a small gift hidden in a backpack helps make the day special while keeping the cost down.

When my children celebrate birthdays, I make it completely their day. I try to make the world revolve around them (within reason). They particularly enjoy taking overnight trips that allow them to explore one of their interests. For example, my son is into art and inventors, so I took him to a Leonardo da Vinci exhibit and we stayed in a motel.

—Patsy Zettle, mother of four children

Traditions Are Important to Kids

Keep in mind how important family traditions are to your children, even when they're grown up.

When our daughters were young, we started the tradition of making yarn trails for Easter. Aubri and Brooke each took the end of a piece of yarn and gradually wound it up, following the trail under tables and through swing sets until they reached their Easter baskets. Last year, my husband and I made plans to go out of town for Easter. The girls, then twenty-one and twenty-four and living on their own, complained that it would be the first year without the yarn trail. So, we strung yarn throughout the house before leaving and told them to come over on Easter to find their baskets.

—Laurie Keleman, airplane pilot

Traditions with a Twist

Traditions are important because they give your children a sense of ritual and stability. Every so often, show your creative side by doing things a little differently. Fun variations can make traditions even more meaningful to your kids.

I remember one Christmas when my daughter Lauren was five years old, and Sheraton had just built a new hotel in downtown Seattle. We spent Christmas at the new hotel, getting room service and going to their holiday buffet. Lauren is twenty now, and she still talks about that Christmas.

—Deborah Collins, transfer-site operator

Spontaneous Parties

For most children, serving cake and ice cream constitutes a party. The next time you see a cake on sale at the bakery, buy it and come up with a reason to celebrate. You could show your kids the cake and say "Let's find a reason to have a party!"

Our grocery store has a shelf with day-old bakery products. Recently, I noticed an elaborately decorated cake reduced from twelve dollars to three dollars with "Congratulations Dan" written on it. My husband's name is Dan, so I bought the cake. That night, the kids and I made a list of all his positive qualities and congratulated him on being such great guy.

—Lisa Mckinnell

Unique Holiday Celebrations

Whenever you celebrate a holiday, look for ways to insert special meaning into the event. Don't be afraid to stray from traditional commercial routines. Halloween can be an opportunity to dress up and collect candy, but it can also be a time to collect money for UNICEF.

Every Easter, our family members individually write ten things they appreciate about each family member. We ask the kids to be truthful and sincere. They've written things like "I appreciate your sense of humor" and "You help me when I feel sick." When our teenager gets his lists, he is much more agreeable for days afterward. I cherish the lists, and my family does, too.

—Patricia Hooley, educator

Surprise Gift

Occasionally surprise your children with an extraordinary gift or experience.

When my boys were three and eight, we spent an incredible weekend together while my wife was away visiting friends. I told the boys I was going to a friend's house to play cards, and that they would have to come along. They weren't very happy. Secretly, I had purchased three tickets to a Michael Jackson concert—they were big fans. We got in the car and started driving, and as we approached the place where Michael Jackson was scheduled to perform, they started roaring. We had the greatest time. They both consider it the highlight of their childhood.

—Doug Stadtmiller, roller-skating center manager

Special Birthday Decorations

Many adults dread the thought of facing another birthday, but children eagerly look forward to their special days. Kids love the hoopla and parties and presents and cake. Get your children off to a memorable start by decorating their bedrooms while they sleep. Some families celebrate by having other family members wake up the birthday child with a lively rendition of "Happy Birthday."

The night before my daughter's birthday, I decorate the house while she's asleep. She wakes up to balloons, flowers, and streamers greeting her on her special day.

—Mother and economist

Teach Respect for Special Occasions

Encourage your children to formally recognize special occasions that may not directly involve them. Ask your children's advice on what present to buy Grandma for Mother's Day, or have your kids wrap a cousin's graduation present. You can teach your children important social skills by encouraging them to focus on what's happening in other people's lives.

I make a point of keeping my children informed about their relatives' graduations, weddings, and other special events. Even if my kids aren't close to the cousin who's having a birthday, I want them to appreciate the rules of etiquette.

—*Samantha Billings, nurse*

Explain the Significance of Holidays

Take time to explain to your children the history behind holidays. Tell them stories about how you celebrated Hanukkah or Christmas when you were a child. If Grandma and Grandpa are celebrating their fortieth wedding anniversary, help your children understand how their grandparents' marriage produced other families. Children benefit from knowing the reasons behind special events.

Every Mother's Day, I give my boys a present thanking them for making me a mother.

—Christine Koplowitz, mother of four sons

Invite Special Guests to Ordinary Events

Sometimes an ordinary event becomes extraordinary when special guests are invited. Give your children a thrill by inviting friends or grandparents to school plays or soccer games.

My daughters Bronwyn and Gylany love tea parties. So, I decided to host an extraspecial tea party by inviting their two grandmothers. The girls dressed in their finest outfits complete with white gloves. One grandmother arrived wearing a fifties outfit complete with leopard-skin dress and cat-eye glasses. The other grandmother wore a colorful dress with a fox stole. Everyone drank tea, ate finger sandwiches, posed for pictures, and enjoyed a memorable afternoon.

—Sandy Ferringer, designer

Add Excitement to Everyday Routines

Children love surprises. Yes, a pony makes a nice surprise, but there are less expensive ways to add excitement to everyday routines. Follow the simplicity trend and look for easy, inexpensive ways to let your children know they're valued members of the family.

When we go out to dinner as a family on Friday night, we almost always have to wait in line. To add some excitement and enjoy some family fun, we reserve our table under one of our children's names. It's great to see their faces when they hear their names announced over the intercom.

—Lisa Jimenez, M.Ed., professional speaker

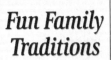

Fun Family Traditions

by Cynthia MacGregor

A book packed with complete directions for fun and meaningful family activities—all designed to strengthen families and to help instill feelings of love, belonging, and family pride.

Order #2446

Practical Parenting Tips

by Vicki Lansky

Here's the #1-selling tricks-of-the-trade book for new parents. Includes tips on toilet training, discipline, travel, temper tantrums, childproofing, and more.

Order # 1180

Discipline without Shouting or Spanking

by Jerry Wyckoff, Ph.D., and Barbara C. Unell

The most practical guide to discipline available, this book provides proven methods for handling the 30 most common forms of childhood misbehavior, from whining and temper tantrums to sibling rivalry.

Order #1079

What Do You Know about Manners?

by Cynthia MacGregor

Here is a book about manners that kids will actually enjoy reading! And their parents will love it too. It's filled with fun, imaginative ways to fine-tune a child's manners and contains over 100 quiz items and hilarious illustrations.

Order #3201

The Toddler's Busy Book

by Trish Kuffner

This book contains 365 activities (one for each day of the year) for toddlers using things found around the home. It shows parents and day-care providers how to prevent boredom, stimulate a child's natural curiosity, and keep toddlers occupied.

Order #1250

The Preschooler's Busy Book

by Trish Kuffner

This book contains 365 activities (one for each day of the year) for three- to six-year-olds using things found around the home. It shows parents and day-care providers how to prevent boredom, stimulate a child's natural curiosity, and keep toddlers occupied.

Order #6055

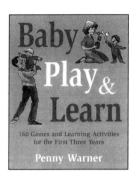

Baby Play & Learn

by Penny Warner

Child development expert Penny Warner offers 160 ideas for games and activities that will provide hours of developmental learning opportunities, including a bulleted list of skills that your baby is learning through play, step-by-step instructions for each game and activity, and illustrations demonstrating how to play many of the games.

Order #1275

Preschooler Play & Learn

by Penny Warner

Child development expert Penny Warner offers 150 ideas for games and activities that will provide hours of developmental learning opportunities, including a bulleted list of skills that your preschooler is learning through play, step-by-step instructions for each game and activity, and illustrations demonstrating how to play many of the games.

Order #1276

Order Form

Qty.	Title	Author	Order No.	Unit Cost (U.S. $)	Total
	Baby/Child Emergency First Aid	Einzig, M.	1381	$8.00	
	Baby & Child Medical Care	Einzig/Hart	1159	$9.00	
	Baby Play & Learn	Warner, P.	1275	$9.00	
	Child Care A to Z	Woolfson, R.	1010	$11.00	
	Childhood Medical Record Book	Fix, S.	1130	$10.00	
	Dads Say the Dumbest Things!	Lansky/Jones	4220	$7.00	
	Discipline w/o Shouting/Spanking	Wykoff/Unell	1079	$6.00	
	Feed Me! I'm Yours	Lansky, V.	1109	$9.00	
	Fun Family Traditions	MacGregor, C.	2446	$9.00	
	Gentle Discipline	Lighter, D.	1085	$6.00	
	Grandma Knows Best	McBride, M.	4009	$7.00	
	How to Read Child Like a Book	Weiss, L.	1145	$8.00	
	Joy of Parenthood	Blaustone, J.	3500	$7.00	
	Moms Say the Funniest Things!	Lansky, B.	4280	$7.00	
	Practical Parenting Tips	Lansky, V.	1180	$8.00	
	Preschooler Play & Learn	Warner, P.	1276	$9.00	
	Preschooler's Busy Book	Kuffner, T.	6055	$9.95	
	Toddler's Busy Book	Kuffner, T.	1250	$9.95	
	What Do You Know about Manners?	MacGregor, C.	3201	$6.99	
				Subtotal	
			Shipping and Handling (see below)		
			MN residents add 6.5% sales tax		
				Total	

YES! Please send me the books indicated above. Add $2.00 shipping and handling for the first book with a retail price up to $9.99 or $3.00 for the first book with a retail price over $9.99. Add $1.00 shipping and handling for each additional book. All orders must be prepaid. Most orders are shipped within two days by U.S. Mail (7–9 delivery days). Rush shipping is available for an extra charge. Overseas postage will be billed.
Quantity discounts available upon request.

Send book(s) to:

Name _____ Address _____

City _____ State _____ Zip _____ Telephone (_____)_____

Payment via:
❑ Check or money order payable to Meadowbrook Press
❑ Visa (for orders over $10.00 only)   ❑ MasterCard (for orders over $10.00 only)
Account # _____ Signature _____ Exp. Date _____

A FREE Meadowbrook Press catalog is available upon request.
You can also phone us for orders of $10.00 or more at 800-338-2232.

Mail to: Meadowbrook Press, 5451 Smetana Drive, Minnetonka, MN 55343
Phone 952-930-1100   Toll-Free 800-338-2232   Fax 952-930-1940
For more information (and fun) visit our website: www.meadowbrookpress.com